KETO
COOKE
FOR BREAKFAST AND
SNACKS

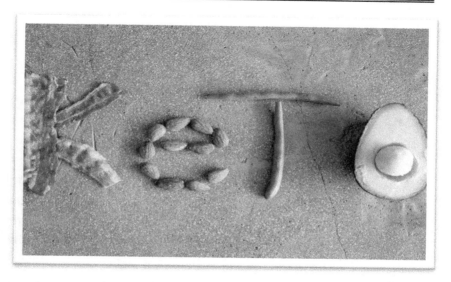

Quick and Easy Low-carb Homemade cooking for Health and Lose-weight

Raven Chook

TABLE OF CONTENT

Where Did the Keto Diet Come From?

The keto diet was introduced in the 1920s to treat children with seizures. It was found that when children were given a fat and low-carbohydrate diet, their seizures stopped.

Later, effective anti-seizure medicines have been created so that the diet has almost vanished. Nevertheless, in 1993, a boy named Charlie was also suffering from seizures, including medications. The hallucinations avoided transitioning to the keto diet. That is how the Charlie Foundation was founded, and the aim of the Foundation is to provide free information on the Keto diet and how it can benefit others. That is also when the keto diet has been resurrected.

"The natural diet is a ketogenic diet. You must do it properly and with a goal."

It promotes foods rich in fat, such as almonds, coconut milk and butter. The diet forbids rice, wheat, sugar and grain intake. The ketones replace glucose as fuel for the body, particularly the brain. This fat metabolism decreases systemic inflammation, which can lead to epilepsy and other conditions. This is also what encourages safe weight loss.

However, before you start eating like this, you need to learn what the keto diet really is, the benefits and the drawbacks of your diet, and whether it is good for you. It has some inconveniences, and it may not be for everyone. We'll look at these more closely later.

What Is the Keto Diet?

Keto diets are diets that produce ketones at its heart. Ketones are formed when so few carbohydrates exist that energy must be extracted when fatty acids are broken down.

A few different diets, including the adapted Atkins diet, the Atkins diet, and the ketogenic diet, fall within this broad umbrella of low carb diets.

You eat very high fat and low carbohydrates in the mainstream, conventional ketogenic diet. The rest is protein. The ratios are roughly 75% fat, 20% protein and just 5% carbohydrates.

The Atkins diet allows only carbohydrates to be counted, which makes maintenance easier. "You're getting 20 or fewer grams, and that's it. The fat and protein count is not regulated."

You do not need to get the majority of your calories from fat with the Atkins diet – you simply limit your carbohydrates. Many people naturally turn to proteins such as meat or fish over fats when they reduce carbohydrates. "That's why you hear people say that high protein is a keto diet," she said.

Atkins' adjusted diet is a cross between the two. You restrict carbohydrates and cannot enjoy protein. Fats, though not as much as with the traditional ketogenic diet, are promoted.

You're still ready to eat what you can and cannot eat, so to speak. First, let's talk about what a ketogenic diet is.

Any diet forces the body into a ketosis process. This is the mechanism in which fats are absorbed by energy rather than by carbohydrates. When done properly, the keto diet needs the dieter to eat high quantities of fats, moderate quantities of protein and very low quantities of carbs.

The bodies normally turn carbohydrates in the traditional diet into glucose, which is sent throughout the body as a source of energy. In the keto diet, we get ketosis that causes our liver to break down fatty cells into fatty acids and ketones to be used as energy.

We eat mainly protein, carbohydrates and some fat in a normal or conventional diet. The additional fat is stored.

You eat more fats, very few carbohydrates, and just enough protein for growth in a ketogenic diet.

When the body produces ketones, fat is used to produce energy. The body produces glucose or blood sugar when you eat carbohydrates.

The body enters a ketosis state when it is on the keto diet. Ketosis is a state of energy in which the body uses alternative fuel to supply energy. Instead of using carbohydrates for fuel, it starts to burn fat.

If you eat a very low level of carbohydrates, you get ketosis which depends on the plan and stage you follow. It's normally 20 grams a day, to start with. Your diet is primarily fat, carbohydrates and green vegetables.

Ketogenic Diets Can Help You Lose Weight

A ketogenic diet is a successful way of losing weight and reducing disease risk factors.

Research indicates that the ketogenic diet is much preferable to the low-fat diet, which is often recommended.

Moreover, the diet is so complete that you can lose weight without counting calories or tracking the consumption of food.

For one study, people who have a ketogenic diet lose 2 times as much weight as people who have a low-fat calorie diet. The cholesterol levels of triglycerides and HDL have increased.

Another research showed that people on the ketogenic diet lose three times the weight of the diet prescribed by Diabetes Great Britain.

There are many reasons that a ketogenic diet is preferable to a fat-free diet, including the increased consumption of protein that provides other benefits.

Increased ketones, lower blood sugar levels and improved response to insulin may also play a crucial role.

Foods to eat on the diet

Wonder what's in a keto diet — and what doesn't? "It is so important to know what foods you're going to consume and how to add more fats to your diet before you start."

Protein

<u>Liberally</u>: (That said, ketogenic diets are not rich in protein and are based on fat and should be moderately eaten.)

Grass-fed beef

Fish, especially fatty fish, like salmon

Dark meat chicken

<u>Occasionally:</u>

Bacon

Low-fat proteins such as shrimp and skinless chicken breast. They are perfect for your keto diet.

<u>Never</u>:

Marinated meat deep in sugary sauces

Chicken nuggets or fish nuggets

Oil and Fat

Heavy cream

Butter

Coconut oil

Avocado oil

Olive oil

Reduce your intake, which you need to do conveniently in order to avoid processed foods, frequently contained in them.

Safflower oil

Corn oil

Sunflower oil

<u>Never</u>:

Margarine

Artificial trans fats

Fruits and Veggies

Celery

Asparagus

Avocado

Leafy greens, like spinach and arugula

<u>Occasionally</u>:

There are all great options, but these carbs do have to be counted.

Eggplant

Leeks

Spaghetti squash

Never:

Raisins

Potatoes

Corn

Nuts and Seeds

Flaxseed and chia seeds

Walnuts

Almonds

Occasionally:

Pistachios

Cashews

almond or peanut butter

Never:

Chocolate-covered nuts

Trail mixes with dried fruit

Sweetened nut or seed butters

Dairy Products

Feta cheese

Cheddar cheese

Blue cheese

Occasionally:

Full-fat ricotta cheese

Full-fat cottage cheese

Full-fat plain Greek yoghurt

Never:

Ice cream

Sweetened nonfat yoghurt

Milk

Sweeteners

Occasionally:

Erythritol

Xylitol

Stevia

Never:

White and brown sugars

Maple syrup

Agave

Honey

Condiments and Sauces

Mayonnaise (no sugar)

Guacamole

Lemon butter sauce

Occasionally:

Tomato sauce (no sugar version)

Balsamic vinegar

Raw garlic

Never:

Ketchup

Barbecue sauce

Honey mustard

Drinks

Plain tea

Almond milk

Water

Bone broth

Occasionally:

Diet soda

Unsweetened carbonated water

Zero-calorie drinks

Black coffee

Never:

Fruit juice

Lemonade

Soda

Herbs and Spices

All herbs and spices fit into a keto diet, but Mancinelli recommends that you count the

carb if you use large amounts.

Thyme, oregano, paprika, and cayenne

Salt (salt foods to taste)

Pepper

Occasionally:

These are all excellent options, but they include some carbs.

Onion powder

Ground ginger

Garlic powder

Never:

Herbs and spices are usually all right to be used to add flavor to food in limited quantities.

Supplements

Multivitamin

Fiber

Optional:

This helps you make ketones easier, but Mancinelli says she doesn't have an opinion to suggest whether you take them or not.

Exogenous ketones

MCT oil

Breakfast Recipes

Bacon Hash

Preparation time: 5 minutes.

Cooking time: 10 minutes.

Servings: 2

Ingredients:

- ❖ 1 small green pepper
- ❖ 2 jalapenos
- ❖ 1 small onion
- ❖ 4 eggs
- ❖ 6 bacon slices

Directions:

1. Chop the bacon into chunks using a food processor. Set aside for now. Slice the peppers and onions into thin strips. Dice the jalapenos as small as possible.

2. Heat a skillet and fry the veggies. Once browned, combine the ingredients and cook until crispy. Place on a serving dish with the eggs.

Nutrition: Carbohydrates: 9g - Protein: 23g - Fats: 24g - Calories: 366

Bagels with Cheese

Preparation time: 10 minutes.

Cooking time: 15 minutes.

Servings: 2

Ingredients:

- ❖ 2.5 cups mozzarella cheese
- ❖ 1 teaspoon baking powder
- ❖ 3 ounces cream cheese
- ❖ 1.5 cups almond flour
- ❖ 2 eggs

Directions:

1. Shred the mozzarella and combine with the flour, baking powder, and cream cheese in a mixing container. Pop into the microwave for about one minute. Mix well.

2. Let the mixture cool and add the eggs. Break apart into six sections and shape into round bagels. Note: You can also sprinkle with a seasoning of your choice or pinch of salt if desired.

3. Bake for approximately 12 minutes. Serve or cool and store.

Nutrition: Carbohydrates: 8g - Protein: 19g - Fats: 31g – Calories: 374

Baked Apples

Preparation time: 10 minutes.

Cooking time: 1 hour.

Servings: 2

Ingredients:

- ❖ 4 teaspoons keto-friendly sweetener.
- ❖ 0.75 teaspoon cinnamon
- ❖ 0.25 cup chopped pecans
- ❖ 4 large granny smith apples

Directions:

1. Set the oven temperature at 375°F. Mix the sweetener with cinnamon and pecans. Core the apple and add the prepared stuffing.

2. Add enough water into the baking dish to cover the bottom of the apple. Bake them for about 45 minutes to 1 hour.

Nutrition: Carbohydrates: 16g - Protein: 6.8g

Fats: 19.9g - Calories: 175

Baked Eggs in the Avocado

Preparation time: 10 minutes.

Cooking time: 20 minutes.

Servings: 1

Ingredients:

- ❖ 1/2 avocado
- ❖ 1 egg
- ❖ 1 tablespoon olive oil

- ❖ 1/2 cup shredded cheddar cheese

Directions:

1. Heat the oven to reach 425°F.

2. Discard the avocado pit and remove just enough of the 'insides' to add the egg. Drizzle with oil and break the egg into the shell.

3. Sprinkle with cheese and bake them for 15 to 16 minutes until the egg is the way you prefer. Serve.

Nutrition: Carbohydrates: 3g- Protein: 21g –

Fats: 52g · Calories: 452

Banana Pancakes

Preparation time: 10 minutes.

Cooking time: 15 minutes.

Servings: 2

Ingredients:

- ❖ Butter
- ❖ 2 bananas

- ❖ 4 eggs

- ❖ 1 teaspoon cinnamon

- ❖ 1 teaspoon baking powder (optional)

Directions:

1. Combine all the ingredients. Melt a portion of butter in a skillet using the medium temperature setting.

2. Prepare the pancakes for 1–2 minutes per side. Cook them with the lid on for the first part of the cooking cycle for a fluffier pancake.

3. Serve plain or with your favorite garnishes, such as a dollop of coconut cream or fresh berries.

Nutrition: Carbohydrates: 6.8g - Total fat: 7g

Calories: 157

Breakfast Skillet

Preparation time: 10 minutes.

Cooking time: 15 minutes.

Servings: 2

Ingredients:

- ❖ 1 pound organic ground turkey/grass-fed beef
- ❖ 6 organic eggs
- ❖ 1 cup keto-friendly salsa of choice

Directions:

1. Warm the skillet using oil (medium heat). Add the turkey and simmer until the pink is gone. Fold in the salsa and simmer for two to three minutes.

2. Crack the eggs and add to the top of the turkey base. Place a lid on the pot and cook for seven minutes until the whites of the eggs are opaque.

3. Note: The cooking time will vary depending on how you like the eggs prepared

Nutrition: Carbohydrates: 7.1g- Protein: 65.2g

Fats: 32g - Calories: 556

Green Banana Pancakes

Preparation time: 20 minutes.

Cooking time: 15 minutes.

Servings: 2

Ingredients

- ❖ 2 large peeled bananas
- ❖ 2 eggs
- ❖ 6 tablespoons of coconut flour
- ❖ 2 teaspoons cassava flour or arrowroot starch
- ❖ Pinch of salt

- ❖ ¼ teaspoon stevia powder
- ❖ 1 tablespoon of baking powder
- ❖ Coconut oil or grass-fed butter

Directions:

1. Puree the banana until smooth.

2. Mix the coconut flour, stevia, arrowroot or cassava, baking soda, and a pinch of salt in a mixing bowl to make a powder form.

3. Whisk egg very lightly in a small bowl, then pour into the banana, mix well.

4. Then add the powder mixture to it. If the mixture is too thick, add some water with a spoon to make it slightly thin; do not over-water.

5. Preheat a skillet along with butter, ghee, or oil.

6. Pour in the batter in the skillet with a spoon.

7. When it is golden brown on top, flip it, cook until brown, and place it on a plate. Serve hot.

Nutrition: Calories: 224 - Cholesterol: 224mg

Total Fat: 32g - Total Carbs: 5g

Berry Bread Spread

Preparation time: 15 minutes.

Cooking time: 15 minutes.

Servings: 2

Ingredients

- ❖ 2 cups coconut cream
- ❖ 2 ounces strawberries
- ❖ 1(½) ounce blueberries
- ❖ 1(½) ounce raspberries

❖ ½ teaspoon coconut extract

Directions:

1. Dice three of each berry in small pieces separately.

2. Blend the remaining strawberries, blueberries, and raspberries in a blender until smooth.

3. Mix in the coconut extract and coconut cream.

4. Blend again until smooth, then add the diced berries.

5. Serve chilled.

Nutrition: Calories 285 - Total Fat 18g

Total Carbs 5.5g - Protein: 6.8g

Chocolate Bread Spread

Preparation time: 15 minutes.

Cooking time: 15 minutes.

Servings: 2

Ingredients

- ❖ 4 cups of sweet cream
- ❖ 2 ounces of coconut oil
- ❖ 3 ounces of chocolate
- ❖ 1 teaspoon of coconut extract
- ❖ 1 tablespoon of powdered cacao
- ❖ Groundnuts for serving [optional]

Directions:

1. Put sweet cream in a microwavable bowl and heat for 10–15 seconds

2. Add coconut oil and mix, then mix in the chocolate and powdered cacao, mix well.

3. Heat the mixture in the microwave for a minute or so.

4. When it is warm, add groundnuts, if desired. Pour in fridge bowls and chill. Serve as you desire.

Nutrition: Calories: 257 - Total Fat: 19g

Total Carbs:7.5g - Protein: 11.8g

Keto Almond Cereal

Preparation time: 20 minutes.

Cooking time: 5 minutes.

Servings: 2

Ingredients

- ❖ 3 cups of unsweetened coconut flakes
- ❖ 1 cup of sliced almonds
- ❖ ¾ tablespoon of cinnamon
- ❖ ¾ tablespoon of nutmeg

Directions:

1. Preheat the oven to 250ºF.

2. Mix the almonds and coconut flakes together, then add nutmeg and cinnamon. Mix well.

3. Spread the nut mixture on a baking tray, and bake for 3–5 minutes.

4. Take out when slightly brown.

5. Enjoy with milk.

Nutrition: Calories: 104- Fat: 15g - Carbohydrates: 4g - Protein: 5g

Keto Granola Cereal

Preparation time: 30 minutes.

Cooking time: 5 minutes.

Servings: 2

Ingredients

- ❖ 1 cup of flaxseeds
- ❖ 1 large egg
- ❖ 1 cup almonds
- ❖ 1 cup hazelnuts
- ❖ 1 cup pecans

- ❖ 1/3 cup pumpkin seeds
- ❖ 1/3 cup sunflower seeds
- ❖ 1/4 cup melted butter/ coconut oil/ ghee for dairy-free
- ❖ 1 teaspoon vanilla extract

Directions:

1. Preheat the oven to 370ºF, and line the baking drays with wax or parchment paper.

2. Pulse almonds and hazelnuts in a food processor intermittently, until chopped into large pieces, then add pecans and chop again into large pieces. Pecans are added later since they are softer.

3. Add the pumpkin seeds, sunflower seeds, and flaxseeds, and pulse just until everything is mixed well. Don't over-process; you should have most seeds in intact form.

4. Whisk an egg white and pour it into the food processor.

5. Then whisk together the melted butter and vanilla extract in a small bowl, and evenly pour that in the food processor, too.

6. Pulse again to mix well until it combines in the form of coarse meal and nut pieces, and everything

should be a little moist from the egg white and butter.

7. Transfer the mixture to the baking tray, evenly pressing, bake for 15 to 18 minutes, or until slightly brown from the edges.

8. Let it cool.

9. Break it into pieces.

Nutrition: Calories: 441 - Fat: 40g Carbohydrates: 4g - Protein: 16g

Sesame-Keto Bagels

Preparation time: 10 minutes.

Cooking time: 15 minutes.

Servings: 2

Ingredients:

- ❖ 2 cups almond flour
- ❖ 3 eggs
- ❖ 1 tablespoon baking powder
- ❖ 2(½) cups mozzarella cheese, shredded
- ❖ ½ cream cheese, cubed
- ❖ 1 pinch salt

❖ 2–3 teaspoons sesame seeds

Directions:

1. Preheat the oven to 425°F.

2. Use a medium bowl to whisk the almond flour and baking powder. Add the mozzarella cheese and cubed cream cheese into a large bowl, mix, and microwave for 90 seconds. Place 2 eggs into the almond mixture and stir thoroughly to form a dough.

3. Part your dough into 6 portions and make it into balls. Press every dough ball slightly to make a hole in the center and put your ball on the baking mat.

4. Brush the top of every bagel with the remaining egg and the top with sesame seeds.

5. Bake for about 15 minutes.

Nutrition: Carbohydrates: 9g - Fat: 39g

Protein: 23g - Calories: 469

Baked Eggs in Avocado Halves

Preparation time: 10 minutes.

Cooking time: 15 minutes.

Servings: 2

Ingredients:

- ❖ 1 large avocado
- ❖ 2 eggs
- ❖ 3 ounces bacon
- ❖ 1 small tomato, chopped
- ❖ 1 pinch salt and paper

❖ ½ ounce lettuce, shredded

Directions:

1. Fry the bacon and cut it. Put aside.

2. Warm your oven to 375°F.

3. Cut the avocado into two halves and make a large hole in each half to place the egg in it.

4. Put avocado halves onto a baking sheet, place eggs, add salt and pepper. Cover the eggs with chopped tomatoes and bacon.

5. Bake for 15 minutes and top your avocadoes with shredded lettuce at the end.

Nutrition: Carbohydrates: 7g - Fat: 72g

Protein: 26g - Calories: 810

Spicy-Cream Cheese Pancakes

Preparation time: 15 minutes.

Cooking time: 20 minutes.

Servings: 2

Ingredients:

- ❖ 3 eggs
- ❖ 9 tablespoons cottage cheese
- ❖ Salt to taste
- ❖ ½ tablespoons psyllium husk powder

- ❖ Butter, for frying
- ❖ 4 ounces cream cheese
- ❖ 1 tablespoon green pesto
- ❖ 1 tablespoon olive oil
- ❖ ¼ red onion, finely sliced
- ❖ Black pepper to taste

Directions:

1. Combine cream cheese, olive oil, and pesto. Put this mixture aside.

2. Blend eggs, psyllium husk powder, cottage cheese, and salt until the mixture is smooth. Leave it for 5 minutes.

3. Heat the butter in the pan and put several dollops of cottage cheese batter into the pan. Fry for a few minutes on each side.

4. Top your pancakes with a large amount of cream cheese mixture and several red onion slices.

5. Add black pepper and olive oil.

Nutrition: Carbohydrates: 7g - Fat: 38g

Protein: 18g - Calories: 449

Bracing-Ginger Smoothie

Preparation time: 5 minutes.

Cooking time: 5 minutes.

Servings: 2

Ingredients:

- ❖ 1/3 cup coconut cream
- ❖ 2/3 cup water
- ❖ 2 tablespoons lime juice
- ❖ 1-ounce spinach, frozen
- ❖ 2 tablespoons ginger, grated

Directions:

1. Blend all the ingredients. Add 1 tablespoon of lime at first and increase the amount if necessary.

2. Top with grated ginger and enjoy your smoothie!

Nutrition: Carbohydrates: 3g - Fat: 8g

Protein: 1g - Calories: 82

Morning-Coffee with Cream

Preparation time: 0 minutes.

Cooking time: 5 minutes.

Servings: 1

Ingredients:

- ❖ ¾ cup coffee
- ❖ ¼ cup whipping cream

Directions:

1. Make your favorite coffee.

2. Put heavy cream in a saucepan and heat slowly until you get a frothy texture.

3. Pour the hot cream into a big cup, add coffee and enjoy your morning drink.

Nutrition: Carbohydrates: 2g - Fat: 21g

Protein: 2g - Calories: 202

Egg-Crust Pizza

Preparation time: 5 minutes.

Cooking time: 15 minutes.

Servings: 1–2

Ingredients

- ❖ ¼ teaspoon of dried oregano to taste
- ❖ ½ teaspoon of spike seasoning to taste
- ❖ 1ounce of mozzarella, chopped into small cubes
- ❖ 6–8 sliced thinly black olives
- ❖ 6 slices of turkey pepperoni, sliced into half
- ❖ 4-5 thinly sliced small grape tomatoes

* ❖ 2 eggs, beaten well
* ❖ 1-2 teaspoons of olive oil

Directions:

1. Preheat the broiler in an oven, then in a small bowl, beat well the eggs. Cut the pepperoni and tomatoes into slices, then cut the mozzarella cheese into cubes.

2. Put olive oil in a skillet over medium heat, then heat the pan for around one minute until it begins to get hot. Add eggs and season with oregano and spike seasoning, then cook for around 2 minutes until the eggs begin to set at the bottom.

3. Drizzle half of the mozzarella, olives, pepperoni, and tomatoes over the eggs followed by another layer of the remaining half of the above ingredients. Ensure that there is a lot of cheese on the topmost layers. Cover the skillet using a lid and cook until the cheese begins to melt and the eggs are set for around 3–4 minutes.

4. Place the pan under the preheated broiler and cook until the top has browned and the cheese has melted nicely for around 2–3 minutes. Serve immediately.

Nutrition: Calories: 363g - Fats: 24.1g-
Carbohydrates: 20.8g - Proteins: 19.25g

Breakfast-Roll-Ups

Preparation time: 5 minutes.

Cooking time: 15 minutes.

Servings: 2 roll-ups.

Ingredients

- ❖ Non-stick cooking spray
- ❖ 5 patties of cooked breakfast sausage
- ❖ 5 slices of cooked bacon
- ❖ 1.5 cups of cheddar cheese, shredded
- ❖ Pepper and salt to taste
- ❖ 10 large eggs

Directions:

1. Heat a skillet on medium to high heat, then using a whisk, combine two of the eggs in a mixing bowl.

2. After the pan has become hot, lower the heat to medium-low heat, then put in the eggs. If you want to, you can utilize some cooking spray.

3. Season eggs with some pepper and salt.

4. Cover eggs, leave them to cook for a couple of minutes or until the eggs are almost cooked.

5. Drizzle around 1/3 cup of cheese on top of the eggs, then place a strip of bacon and divide the sausage into two, and place on top.

6. Roll the egg carefully on top of the fillings. The roll-up will almost look like a taquito. If you have a hard time folding over the egg, use a spatula to keep the egg intact until the egg has molded into a roll-up.

7. Put aside the roll-up, then repeat the above steps until you have four more roll-ups; you should have 5 roll-ups in total.

Nutrition: Calories: 412.2g - Fats: 31.66g

Carbohydrates: 2.26g - Proteins: 28.21g

Basic Opie Rolls

Preparation time: 20 minutes.

Cooking time: 35 minutes.

Servings: 2 rolls.

Ingredients

- ❖ 1/8 teaspoon of salt
- ❖ 1/8 teaspoon of cream of tartar
- ❖ 3 ounces of cream cheese
- ❖ 3 large eggs

Directions:

1. Preheat the oven to about 148.889ºC or 300ºF, then separate the egg whites from egg yolks and place both eggs in different bowls. Using an electric mixer, beat well the egg whites until the mixture is very bubbly, then add the cream of tartar and mix again until it forms a stiff peak.

2. In the bowl with the egg yolks, put 3 ounces of cubed cheese and salt. Mix well until the mixture has doubled in size and is pale yellow. Put the egg white mixture into the egg yolk mixture, then fold the mixture gently together.

3. Spray some oil on the cookie sheet coated with some parchment paper, then add dollops of the batter and bake for around 30 minutes.

4. When the upper part of the rolls is firm and golden, they are ready. Leave them to cool for a few minutes on a wire rack. Enjoy with some coffee.

Nutrition: Calories: 45 - Fats: 4g

Carbohydrates: 0g - Proteins: 2g

Almond Coconut Egg Wraps

Preparation time: 5 minutes.

Cooking time: 5 minutes.

Servings: 2

Ingredients:

- ❖ 5 organic eggs
- ❖ 1 tablespoon coconut flour
- ❖ 0.25 teaspoon sea salt
- ❖ 2 tablespoons almond meal

Directions:

1. Combine all the ingredients in a blender and work them until creamy. Heat a skillet using the med-high temperature setting.

2. Pour two tablespoons of batter into the skillet and cook - covered about three minutes. Turn it over to cook for another 3 minutes. Serve the wraps piping hot.

Bacon & Avocado Omellete

Preparation time: 5 minutes.

Cooking time: 5 minutes.

Servings: 1

Ingredients:

- ❖ 1 slice crispy bacon

- ❖ 2 large organic eggs
- ❖ 5 cup freshly grated parmesan cheese
- ❖ 2 tablespoons ghee or coconut oil or butter
- ❖ 1/2 small avocado

Directions:

1. Prepare the bacon to your liking and set aside. Combine the eggs, parmesan cheese, and your choice of finely chopped herbs. Warm a skillet and add the butter/ghee to melt using the medium-high heat setting. When the pan is hot, whisk and add the eggs.

2. Prepare the omelet working, it towards the middle of the pan for about 30 seconds. When firm, flip, and cook it for another 30 seconds. Arrange the omelet on a plate and garnish it with the crunched bacon bits. Serve with sliced avocado.

Nutrition: Carbohydrates: 3.3g - Protein: 30g

Fats: 63g - Calories: 719

Bacon & Cheese Frittata

Preparation time: 5 minutes.

Cooking time: 5 minutes.

Servings: 2

Ingredients:

- ❖ 1 cup heavy cream
- ❖ 6 eggs
- ❖ 5 crispy slices of bacon
- ❖ 2 chopped green onions
- ❖ 4 ounces cheddar cheese
- ❖ Also Needed: 1 pie plate

Directions:

1. Warm the oven temperature to reach 350ºF.

2. Whisk the eggs and seasonings. Empty into the pie pan and top off with the remaining ingredients. Bake 30–35 minutes. Wait for a few minutes before serving for best results.

Nutrition: Carbohydrates: 2g - Protein: 13g

Fats: 29g - Calories: 320

Bacon and Egg Breakfast Sandwich

Preparation time: 20 minutes.

Cooking time: 8 minutes.

Servings: 2

Ingredients:

- ❖ 2 cups of bell peppers; chopped
- ❖ 1/2 tablespoon of avocado oil
- ❖ 3 eggs
- ❖ 4 bacon slices

Directions:

1. Heat up a pan with the oil over medium-high heat, add bell peppers, stir and cook until they are soft.

2. Heat up another pan over medium heat, add bacon, stir and cook until it's crispy.

3. In a bowl; whisk eggs really well and add them to bell peppers.

4. Cook until eggs are done for about 8 minutes. Divide half of the bacon slices between plates, add eggs, top with bacon slices, and serve.

Nutrition: Calories: 200- Fat: 4g- Fiber: 3g

Carbs: 6g- Protein: 10g

Korma Curry

Preparation time: 10 minutes.

Cooking time: 25 minutes.

Servings: 2

Ingredients:

- ❖ 3-pound chicken breast, skinless, boneless
- ❖ 1 teaspoon of garam masala
- ❖ 1 teaspoon of curry powder
- ❖ 1 tablespoon of apple cider vinegar
- ❖ 1/2 cup of coconut cream
- ❖ 1 cup of organic almond milk
- ❖ 1 teaspoon of ground coriander

- ❖ ¾ teaspoon of ground cardamom
- ❖ 1/2 teaspoon of ginger powder
- ❖ 1/4 teaspoon of cayenne pepper
- ❖ ¾ teaspoon of ground cinnamon
- ❖ 1 tomato, diced
- ❖ 1 teaspoon of avocado oil
- ❖ 1/2 cup of water

Directions:

1. Chop the chicken breast and put it in the saucepan.

2. Add avocado oil and start to cook it over medium heat.

3. Sprinkle the chicken with garam masala, curry powder, apple cider vinegar, ground coriander, cardamom, ginger powder, cayenne pepper, ground cinnamon, and diced tomato. Mix up the ingredients carefully. Cook them for 10 minutes.

4. Add water, coconut cream, and almond milk. Sauté the meat for 10 minutes more.

Nutrition: Calories: 411- Fat: 19.3g- Fiber: 0.9g

Carbs: 6g- Protein: 49.9g

Zucchini Bars

Preparation time: 10 minutes.

Cooking time: 15 minutes.

Servings: 2

Ingredients:

- ❖ 3 zucchini, grated
- ❖ 1/2 white onion, diced
- ❖ 2 teaspoons of butter
- ❖ 3 eggs, whisked
- ❖ 4 tablespoons of coconut flour

- ❖ 1 teaspoon of salt
- ❖ 1/2 teaspoon of ground black pepper
- ❖ 5 ounces of goat cheese, crumbled
- ❖ 4 ounces of Swiss cheese, shredded
- ❖ 1/2 cup of spinach, chopped
- ❖ 1 teaspoon of baking powder
- ❖ 1/2 teaspoon of lemon juice

Directions:

1. In the mixing bowl, mix up together grated zucchini, diced onion, eggs, coconut flour, salt, ground black pepper, crumbled cheese, chopped spinach, baking powder, and lemon juice.

2. Add butter and churn the mixture until homogenous.

3. Line the baking dish with baking paper.

4. Transfer the zucchini mixture into the baking dish and flatten it.

5. Preheat the oven to 365ºF and put the dish inside.

6. Cook it for 15 minutes. Then chill the meal well. Cut it into bars.

Nutrition: Calories: 199- Fat: 1316g

Fiber: 215g- Carbs: 7.1g- Protein: 13.1g

Mushroom Soup

Preparation time: 10 minutes.

Cooking time: 25 minutes.

Servings: 2

Ingredients:

- ❖ 1 cup of water
- ❖ 1 cup of coconut milk
- ❖ 1 cup of white mushrooms, chopped
- ❖ 1/2 carrot, chopped
- ❖ 1/4 white onion, diced
- ❖ 1 tablespoon of butter
- ❖ 2 ounces turnip, chopped

- ❖ 1 teaspoon of dried dill
- ❖ 1/2 teaspoon of ground black pepper
- ❖ ¾ teaspoon of smoked paprika
- ❖ 1-ounce of celery stalk, chopped

Directions:

1. Pour water and coconut milk into the saucepan. Bring the liquid to a boil.

2. Add chopped mushrooms, carrot, and turnip. Close the lid and boil for 10 minutes.

3. Meanwhile, put butter in the skillet. Add diced onion. Sprinkle it with dill, ground black pepper, and smoked paprika. Roast the onion for 3 minutes.

4. Add the roasted onion to the soup mixture.

5. Then add chopped celery stalk. Close the lid.

6. Cook soup for 10 minutes.

7. Then ladle it into the serving bowls.

Nutrition: Calories: 181- Fat: 17.3g- Fiber: 2.5g- Carbs: 6.9g- Protein: 2.4g

Stuffed Portobello Mushrooms

Preparation time: 10 minutes.

Cooking time: 10 minutes.

Servings: 2

Ingredients:

- ❖ 2 Portobello mushrooms
- ❖ 1 cup of spinach, chopped, steamed
- ❖ 2ounces of artichoke hearts, drained, chopped
- ❖ 1 tablespoon of coconut cream
- ❖ 1 tablespoon of cream cheese

- ❖ 1 teaspoon of minced garlic
- ❖ 1 tablespoon of fresh cilantro, chopped
- ❖ 3 ounces of Cheddar cheese, grated
- ❖ 1/2 teaspoon of ground black pepper
- ❖ 2 tablespoons of olive oil
- ❖ 1/2 teaspoon of salt

Directions:

1. Sprinkle mushrooms with olive oil and place them in the tray.

2. Transfer the tray in the preheated to 360ºF oven and broil them for 5 minutes.

3. Meanwhile, blend together artichoke hearts, coconut cream, cream cheese, minced garlic, and chopped cilantro.

4. Add grated cheese in the mixture and sprinkle with ground black pepper and salt.

5. Fill the broiled mushrooms with the cheese mixture and cook them for 5 minutes more. Serve the mushrooms only hot.

Nutrition: Calories: 183- Fat: 16.3g- Fiber: 1.9g

Carbs: 3g- Protein: 7.7g

Lettuce Salad

Preparation time: 10 minutes.

Cooking time : 10 minutes

Servings: 1

Ingredients:

- ❖ 1 cup of Romaine lettuce, roughly chopped
- ❖ 3 ounces of seitan, chopped
- ❖ 1 tablespoon of avocado oil
- ❖ 1 teaspoon of sunflower seeds
- ❖ 1 teaspoon of lemon juice
- ❖ 1 egg, boiled, peeled
- ❖ 2 ounces of Cheddar cheese, shredded

Directions:

1. Place lettuce in the salad bowl. Add chopped seitan and shredded cheese.

2. Then chop the egg roughly and add to the salad bowl too.

3. Mix up together lemon juice with the avocado oil.

4. Sprinkle the salad with the oil mixture and sunflower seeds. Don't stir the salad before serving.

Nutrition: Calories: 663- Fat: 29.5g

Fiber: 4.7g- Carbs: 3.8g- Protein: 84.2g

Onion Soup

Preparation time: 10 minutes.

Cooking time: 25 minutes.

Servings: 2

Ingredients:

- ❖ 2 cups of white onion, diced
- ❖ 4 tablespoons of butter
- ❖ 1/2 cup of white mushrooms, chopped
- ❖ 3 cups of water
- ❖ 1 cup of heavy cream
- ❖ 1 teaspoon of salt
- ❖ 1 teaspoon of chili flakes
- ❖ 1 teaspoon of garlic powder

Directions:

1. Put butter in the saucepan and melt it.

2. Add diced white onion, chili flakes, and garlic powder. Mix it up and sauté for 10 minutes over medium-low heat.

3. Then add water, heavy cream, and chopped mushrooms. Close the lid.

4. Cook the soup for 15 minutes more.

5. Then blend the soup until you get the creamy texture. Ladle it in the bowls.

Nutrition: Calories: 155- Fat: 15.1g

Fiber: 0.9g- Carbs: 4.7g- Protein: 1.2g

Asparagus Salad

Preparation time: 10 minutes.

Cooking time: 15 minutes.

Servings: 2

Ingredients:

- ❖ 10 ounces of asparagus
- ❖ 1 tablespoon of olive oil
- ❖ 1/2 teaspoon of white pepper
- ❖ 4 ounces of Feta cheese, crumbled
- ❖ 1 cup of lettuce, chopped
- ❖ 1 tablespoon of canola oil
- ❖ 1 teaspoon of apple cider vinegar

❖ 1 tomato, diced

Directions:

1. Preheat the oven to 365ºF.

2. Place asparagus in the tray, sprinkle with olive oil and white pepper and transfer in the preheated oven. Cook it for 15 minutes.

3. Meanwhile, put crumbled Feta in the salad bowl.

4. Add chopped lettuce and diced tomato.

5. Sprinkle the ingredients with apple cider vinegar.

6. Chill the cooked asparagus to room temperature and add the salad.

7. Shake the salad gently before serving.

Nutrition: Calories: 207- Fat: 17.6g

Fiber: 2.4g- Carbs: 6.8g- Protein: 7.8g

Cheesy Breakfast Muffins

Preparation time: 15 minutes.

Cooking time: 12 minutes.

Servings: 2

Ingredients:

- ❖ 4 tablespoons melted butter
- ❖ 3/4 tablespoon baking powder
- ❖ 1 cup almond flour
- ❖ 2 large eggs, lightly beaten
- ❖ 2 ounces cream cheese mixed with 2 tablespoons heavy whipping cream
- ❖ A handful of shredded Mexican blend cheese

Directions:

1. Preheat the oven to 400°F. Grease 6 muffin tin cups with melted butter and set aside.

2. Combine the baking powder and almond flour in a bowl. Stir well and set aside.

3. Stir together 4 tablespoons of melted butter, eggs, shredded cheese, and cream cheese in a separate bowl.

4. The egg and the dry mixture must be combined using a hand mixer to beat until it is creamy and well blended.

5. The mixture must be scooped into the greased muffin cups evenly.

6. Baking time: 12 minutes.

Nutrition: Calories: 214 - Fat: 15.6g - Fiber: 3.1g

Carbohydrates: 5.1g - Protein: 9.5g

Spinach, Mushroom, and Goat Cheese Frittata

Preparation time: 15 minutes.

Cooking time: 20 minutes.

Servings: 2

Ingredients:

- ❖ 2 tablespoons olive oil
- ❖ 1 cup fresh mushrooms, sliced
- ❖ 6 bacon slices, cooked and chopped
- ❖ 1 cup spinach, shredded
- ❖ 10 large eggs, beaten
- ❖ 1/2 cup goat cheese, crumbled
- ❖ Pepper and salt to taste

Directions:

1. Preheat the oven to 350°F.

2. Heat oil and add the mushrooms and fry for 3 minutes until they start to brown, stirring frequently.

3. Fold in the bacon and spinach and cook for about 1 to 2 minutes, or until the spinach is wilted.

4. Slowly pour in the beaten eggs and cook for 3 to 4 minutes. Making use of a spatula, lift the edges for allowing the uncooked egg to flow underneath.

5. Top with the goat cheese and then sprinkle the salt and pepper to season.

6. Bake in the preheated oven for about 15 minutes until lightly golden brown around the edges.

Nutrition: Calories: 265 - Fat: 11.6g - Fiber: 8.6g

Carbohydrates: 5.1g - Protein: 12.9g

Yogurt Waffles

Preparation time: 15 minutes.

Cooking time: 25 minutes.

Servings: 2

Ingredients:

- ❖ 1/2 cup golden flax seeds meal
- ❖ 1/2 cup plus 3 tablespoons almond flour
- ❖ 1–1(1/2) tablespoons granulated Erythritol
- ❖ 1 tablespoon unsweetened vanilla whey protein powder
- ❖ 1/4 teaspoon baking soda
- ❖ 1/2 teaspoon organic baking powder
- ❖ 1/4 teaspoon xanthan gum
- ❖ Salt, as required
- ❖ 1 large organic egg, white and yolk separated
- ❖ 1 organic whole egg
- ❖ 2 tablespoons unsweetened almond milk

- ❖ 1(1/2) tablespoons unsalted butter
- ❖ 3 ounces plain Greek yogurt

Directions:

1. Preheat the waffle iron and then grease it.

2. In a large bowl, add the flour, Erythritol, protein powder, baking soda, baking powder, xanthan gum, salt, and mix until well combined.

3. In another bowl or container, put the egg white and beat until stiff peaks form.

4. In a third bowl, add two egg yolks, whole egg, almond milk, butter, yogurt, and beat until well combined.

5. Place egg mixture into the bowl of the flour mixture and mix until well combined.

6. Gently fold in the beaten egg whites.

7. Place 1/4 cup of the mixture into preheated waffle iron and cook for about 4–5 minutes or until golden brown.

8. Repeat with the remaining mixture.

9. Serve warm.

Nutrition: Calories: 265 - Fat: 11.5g - Fiber: 9.5g

Carbohydrates: 5.2g - Protein: 7.5g

Green Vegetable Quiche

Preparation time: 20 minutes.

Cooking time: 20 minutes.

Servings: 2

Ingredients:

- ❖ 6 organic eggs
- ❖ 1/2 cup unsweetened almond milk
- ❖ Salt and ground black pepper, as required
- ❖ 2 cups fresh baby spinach, chopped
- ❖ 1/2 cup green bell pepper, seeded and chopped
- ❖ 1 scallion, chopped
- ❖ 1/4 cup fresh cilantro, chopped
- ❖ 1 tablespoon fresh chives, minced
- ❖ 3 tablespoons mozzarella cheese, grated

Directions:

1. Preheat your oven to 400ºF.

2. Lightly grease a pie dish.

3. In a bowl, add eggs, almond milk, salt, and black pepper, and beat until well combined. Set aside.

4. In another bowl, add the vegetables and herbs and mix well.

5. At the bottom of the prepared pie dish, place the veggie mixture evenly and top with the egg mixture.

6. Let the quiche bake for about 20 minutes.

7. Remove the pie dish from the oven and immediately sprinkle it with the Parmesan cheese.

8. Set aside for about 5 minutes before slicing.

9. Cut into desired-sized wedges and serve warm.

Nutrition: Calories: 298 - Fat: 10.4g - Fiber: 5.9g

Carbohydrates: 4.1g - Protein: 7.9g

Cheesy Broccoli Muffins

Preparation time: 15 minutes.

Cooking time: 20 minutes.

Servings: 2

Ingredients:

- ❖ 2 tablespoons unsalted butter
- ❖ 6 large organic eggs
- ❖ 1/2 cup heavy whipping cream
- ❖ 1/2 cup Parmesan cheese, grated
- ❖ Salt and ground black pepper, as required
- ❖ 1(1/4) cups broccoli, chopped
- ❖ 2 tablespoons fresh parsley, chopped
- ❖ 1/2 cup Swiss cheese, grated

Directions:

1. Grease a 12-cup muffin tin.

2. In a bowl or container, put the cream, eggs, Parmesan cheese, salt, and black pepper, and beat until well combined.

3. Divide the broccoli and parsley in the bottom of each prepared muffin cup evenly.

4. Top with the egg mixture, followed by the Swiss cheese.

5. Let the muffins bake for about 20 minutes, rotating the pan once halfway through.

6. Carefully, invert the muffins onto a serving platter and serve warm.

Nutrition: Calories: 241 · Fat: 11.5g · Fiber: 8.5g

Carbohydrates: 4.1g - Protein: 11.1g

Berry Chocolate Breakfast Bowl

Preparation time: 10 minutes.

Cooking time: 0 minutes.

Servings: 2

Ingredients:

- ❖ 1/2 cup strawberries, fresh or frozen
- ❖ 1/2 cup blueberries, fresh or frozen
- ❖ 1 cup unsweetened almond milk
- ❖ Sugar-free maple syrup to taste
- ❖ 2 tablespoons unsweetened cocoa powder

❖ 1 tablespoon cashew nuts for topping

Directions:

1. The berries must be divided into four bowls, pour on the almond milk.

2. Drizzle with the maple syrup and sprinkle the cocoa powder on top, a tablespoon per bowl.

3. Top with the cashew nuts and enjoy immediately.

Nutrition: Calories: 287 - Fat: 5.9g - Fiber: 11.4g

Carbohydrates: 3.1 g - Protein: 4.2g

Coco-Nut" Granola

Preparation time: 10 minutes.

Cooking time: 60 minutes.

Servings: 2

Ingredients:

- ❖ 2 cups shredded unsweetened coconut
- ❖ 1 cup sliced almonds
- ❖ 1 cup raw sunflower seeds
- ❖ 1/2 cup raw pumpkin seeds
- ❖ 1/2 cup walnuts
- ❖ 1/2 cup melted coconut oil

- ❖ 10 drops liquid stevia
- ❖ 1 teaspoon ground cinnamon
- ❖ 1/2 teaspoon ground nutmeg

Directions:

1. Preheat the oven to 250°F. Line 2 baking sheets with parchment paper. Set aside.

2. Toss all the ingredients together.

3. The granola will then put into baking sheets and spread out evenly.

4. Bake the granola for about 1 hour.

Nutrition: Calories: 131 - Fat: 4.1g - Fiber: 5.8g

Carbohydrates: 2.8g - Protein: 5.6g

Bacon Artichoke Omelet

Preparation time: 10 minutes.

Cooking time: 10 minutes.

Servings: 2

Ingredients:

- ❖ 6 eggs, beaten
- ❖ 2 tablespoons heavy (whipping) cream
- ❖ 8 bacon slices, cooked and chopped
- ❖ 1 tablespoon olive oil
- ❖ 1/4 cup chopped onion
- ❖ 1/2 cup chopped artichoke hearts (canned, packed in water)
- ❖ Sea salt to taste
- ❖ Freshly ground black pepper to taste

Directions:

1. In a bowl or container, the eggs, heavy cream, and bacon must be mixed.

2. Heat olive oil then sauté the onion until tender, about 3 minutes.

3. Pour the egg mixture into the skillet for 1 minute.

4. Cook the omelet, lifting the edges with a spatula to let the uncooked egg flow underneath for 2 minutes.

5. Sprinkle the artichoke hearts on top and flip the omelet.

6. Cook for 4 minutes more until the egg is firm.

7. Flip the omelet over again, so the artichoke hearts are on top.

8. Remove from the heat, cut the omelet into quarters, and season with salt and black pepper.

9. Transfer the omelet to plates and serve.

Nutrition: Calories: 314 - Fat: 7.1g - Fiber: 5.4g

Carbohydrates: 3.1g - Protein: 8.5g

Spinach-Mushroom Frittata

Preparation time: 10 minutes.

Cooking time: 15 minutes.

Servings: 2

Ingredients:

- ❖ 2 tablespoons olive oil
- ❖ 1 cup sliced fresh mushrooms
- ❖ 1 cup shredded spinach
- ❖ 6 bacon slices, cooked and chopped
- ❖ 10 large eggs, beaten
- ❖ 1/2 cup crumbled goat cheese
- ❖ Sea salt to taste
- ❖ Freshly ground black pepper to taste

Directions:

1. Preheat the oven to 350°F.

2. Heat olive oil and sauté the mushrooms until lightly browned for about 3 minutes.

3. Add the spinach and bacon and sauté until the greens are wilted for about 1 minute.

4. Add the eggs and cook, lifting the edges of the frittata with a spatula so uncooked egg flow underneath for 3 to 4 minutes.

5. Sprinkle with crumbled goat cheese and season lightly with salt and pepper.

6. Bake until set and lightly browned, about 15 minutes.

7. Remove the frittata from the oven and let it stand for 5 minutes.

8. Cut into six wedges and serve immediately.

Nutrition: Calories: 312 - Fat: 6.8g - Fiber: 5.1g

Carbohydrates: 3.1g - Protein: 10.5g

Crêpes with Lemon-Buttery Syrup

Preparation time: 15 minutes.

Cooking time: 20 minutes.

Servings: 2

Ingredients:

- ❖ 6 ounces mascarpone cheese, softened
- ❖ 6 eggs
- ❖ 1(1/2) tablespoon granulated swerve
- ❖ 1/4 cup almond flour
- ❖ 1 teaspoon baking soda
- ❖ 1 teaspoon baking powder

For the Syrup

- ❖ 3/4 cup of water
- ❖ 2 tablespoons lemon juice
- ❖ 1 tablespoon butter
- ❖ 3/4 cup swerve, powdered
- ❖ 1 tablespoon vanilla extract
- ❖ 1/2 teaspoon xanthan gum

Directions:

1. With the use of an electric mixer, mix all the crepes ingredients until well incorporated.

2. Use melted butter to grease a frying pan and set over medium heat; cook the crepes.

3. Flip over and cook the other side for a further 2 minutes; repeat the remaining batter.

4. Put the crepes on a plate.

5. In the same pan, mix swerve, butter and water; simmer for 6 minutes as you stir.

6. Transfer the mixture to a blender and a 1/4 teaspoon of xanthan gum and vanilla extract and mix well.

7. Place in the remaining 1/4 teaspoon of xanthan gum and allow sitting until the syrup is thick.

Nutrition: Calories: 312 - Fat: 11.5g -Fiber: 3.8g

Carbohydrates: 2.4g -Protein: 5.1g

Flaxseed, Maple & Pumpkin Muffin

Preparation time: 10 minutes.

Cooking time: 30 minutes.

Servings: 2

Ingredients:

- ❖ 1 tablespoon cinnamon
- ❖ 1 cup pure pumpkin puree
- ❖ 1 tablespoon pumpkin pie spice

- ❖ 2 tablespoons coconut oil
- ❖ 1 egg
- ❖ 1/2 tablespoon baking powder
- ❖ 1/2 teaspoon salt
- ❖ 1/2 teaspoon apple cider vinegar
- ❖ 1/2 teaspoon vanilla extract
- ❖ 1/3 cup erythritol
- ❖ 1(1/4) cup flaxseeds (ground)
- ❖ 1/4 cup maple syrup

Directions:

1. Line ten muffin tins with ten muffin liners and preheat the oven to 350ºF.

2. All the ingredients must be blended until smooth and creamy, around 5 minutes.

3. Evenly divide batter into prepared muffin tins.

4. Pop in the oven and let it bake for 20 minutes or until tops are lightly browned.

5. Let it cool. Evenly divide into suggested servings and place in meal prep containers.

Nutrition: Calories: 241 · Fat: 11.3g · Fiber: 15.9g

Carbohydrates: 3.1g -Protein: 8.9g

Onion Cheese Muffins

Preparation time: 15 minutes.

Cooking time: 20 minutes.

Servings: 2

Ingredients:

- ❖ 1/4 cup Colby jack cheese, shredded
- ❖ 1/4 cup shallots, minced
- ❖ 1/2 teaspoon salt
- ❖ 1 cup almond flour
- ❖ 1 egg
- ❖ 3 tablespoons melted butter
- ❖ 3 tablespoons sour cream

Directions:

1. Line 6 muffin tins with six muffin liners. Set aside and preheat the oven to 350ºF.

2. In a bowl, stir the dry and wet ingredients alternately. Mix well.

3. Scoop a spoonful of the batter to the prepared muffin tins.

4. Bake for 20 minutes in the oven until golden brown.

Nutrition: Calories: 241 - Fat: 5.1g -Fiber: 2.6g

Carbohydrates: 3.1g - Protein: 4.2g

Cajun Crabmeat Frittata

Preparation time: 15 minutes.

Cooking time: 20 minutes.

Servings: 2

Ingredients:

- ❖ 1 tablespoon olive oil
- ❖ 1 onion, chopped
- ❖ 4 ounces crabmeat, chopped
- ❖ 1 teaspoon Cajun seasoning
- ❖ 6 large eggs, slightly beaten
- ❖ 1/2 cup Greek yogurt

Directions:

1. Let the oven preheat to 350°F/175°C, then set a large skillet over medium heat and warm the oil.

2. Add onion and sauté until soft; place in crabmeat and cook for two more minutes.

3. Season with Cajun seasoning.

4. Evenly distribute the ingredients at the bottom of the skillet.

5. Whisk the eggs with yogurt.

6. Transfer to the skillet.

7. Put it in the oven and let the frittata bake for about 18 minutes or until eggs are cooked.

8. Slice into wedges and serve warm.

Nutrition: Calories: 256 - Fat: 4.9g - Fiber: 2.9g

Carbohydrates: 3.1g - Protein: 8.9g

Snacks Recipes

Fried Green Beans
Rosemary

Preparation time: 10 minutes.

Cooking time: 5 minutes.

Servings: 2

Ingredients:

- ❖ ¾ cup green beans
- ❖ 3 teaspoons minced garlic
- ❖ 2 tablespoons rosemary
- ❖ ½ teaspoon salt

❖ 1 tablespoon butter

Directions:

1. Warm-up an air fryer to 390°F.

2. Put the chopped green beans, then brush with butter. Sprinkle salt, minced garlic, and rosemary over then cook within 5 minutes. Serve.

Nutrition: Calories: 72- Fat: 6.3g

Protein: 0.7g- Carbs: 4.5g

Crispy Broccoli Pop Corn

Preparation time: 15 minutes.

Cooking time: 10 minutes.

Servings: 2

Ingredients:

- ❖ 2 cups broccoli florets
- ❖ 2 cups coconut flour
- ❖ 4 egg yolks
- ❖ ½ teaspoon salt
- ❖ ½ teaspoon pepper
- ❖ ¼ cup butter

Directions:

1. Dissolve butter and then let it cool. Break the eggs in it.

2. Put coconut flour into the liquid, then put salt and pepper. Mix.

3. Warm-up an air fryer to 400°F. Dip a broccoli floret in the coconut flour mixture and then place it in the air fryer.

4. Cook the broccoli florets for 6 minutes. Serve.

Nutrition: Calories: 202- Fat: 17.5g - Protein: 5.1g
Carbs: 7.8g

Cheesy Cauliflower Croquettes

Preparation time: 10 minutes.

Cooking time: 16 minutes.

Servings: 2

Ingredients:

- ❖ 2 cups cauliflower florets

- ❖ 2 teaspoons garlic
- ❖ ½ cup onion
- ❖ ¾ teaspoon mustard
- ❖ ½ teaspoon salt
- ❖ ½ teaspoon pepper
- ❖ 2 tablespoons butter
- ❖ ¾ cup cheddar cheese

Directions:

1. Microwave the butter. Let it cool.

2. Process the cauliflower florets using a processor. Transfer to a bowl then put chopped onion and cheese.

3. Put minced garlic, mustard, salt, and pepper, then pour melted butter over. Shape the cauliflower batter into medium balls.

4. Warm-up an air fryer to 400°f and cook within 14 minutes. Serve.

Nutrition: Calories: 160 - Fat: 13g

Protein: 6.8g- Carbs: 5.1g

Spinach in Cheese Envelopes

Preparation time: 15 minutes.

Cooking time: 30 minutes.

Servings: 2

Ingredients:

- ❖ 3 cups cream cheese
- ❖ 1(½) cup coconut flour
- ❖ 3 egg yolks
- ❖ 2 eggs
- ❖ ½ cup cheddar cheese
- ❖ 2 cups steamed spinach
- ❖ ¼ teaspoon salt
- ❖ ½ teaspoon pepper
- ❖ ¼ cup onion

Directions:

1. Whisk cream cheese put egg yolks. Stir in coconut flour until becoming soft dough.

2. Put the dough on a flat surface, then roll until thin. Cut the thin dough into 8 squares.

3. Beat the eggs and then place them in a bowl. Put salt, pepper, and grated cheese.

4. Put chopped spinach and onion into the egg batter.

5. Put spinach filling on a square dough, then fold until becoming an envelope. Glue with water.

6. Warm-up an air fryer to 425°F (218°C). Cook within 12 minutes.

7. Remove and serve!

Nutrition: Calories: 365- Fat: 34.6g

Protein: 10.4g - Carbs: 4.4g

Cheesy Mushroom Slices

Preparation time: 8–10 minutes.

Cooking time: 15 minutes.

Servings: 2

Ingredients:

- ❖ 2 cups mushrooms
- ❖ 2 eggs
- ❖ ¾ cup almond flour
- ❖ ½ cup cheddar cheese
- ❖ 2 tablespoons butter
- ❖ ½ teaspoon pepper
- ❖ ¼ teaspoon salt

Directions:

1. Processes chopped mushrooms in a food processor then add eggs, almond flour, and cheddar cheese.

2. Put salt and pepper then pour melted butter into the food processor. Transfer.

3. Warm-up an air fryer to 375°F (191°C).

4. Put the loaf pan on the air fryer's rack then cook within 15 minutes. Slice and serve.

Nutrition: Calories: 365- Fat: 34.6g

Protein: 10.4g- Carbs: 4.4g

Asparagus Fries

Preparation time: 10 minutes.

Cooking time: 10 minutes.

Servings: 2

Ingredients:

- ❖ 10 organic asparagus spears
- ❖ 1 tablespoon organic roasted red pepper
- ❖ ¼ cup almond flour
- ❖ ½ teaspoon garlic powder
- ❖ ½ teaspoon smoked paprika
- ❖ 2 tablespoons parsley
- ❖ ½ cup parmesan cheese, and full-fat

- ❖ 2 organic eggs
- ❖ 3 tablespoons mayonnaise, full-fat

Directions:

1. Warm-up the oven to 425ºF.

2. Process cheese in a food processor, add garlic and parsley, and pulse for 1 minute.

3. Add almond flour, pulse for 30 seconds, transfer, and put paprika.

4. Whisk eggs into a shallow dish.

5. Dip asparagus spears into the egg batter, then coat with parmesan mixture and place it on a baking sheet. Bake in the oven within 10 minutes.

6. Put the mayonnaise in a bowl; add red pepper and whisk, and then chill. Serve with prepared dip.

Nutrition: Calories: 453- Fat: 33.4g

Protein: 19.1g- Net carbs: 5.5g

Kale Chips

Preparation time: 5 minutes.

Cooking time: 12 minutes.

Servings: 2

Ingredients:

- ❖ 1 organic kale
- ❖ 1 tablespoon seasoned salt
- ❖ 2 tablespoons olive oil

Directions:

1. Warm-up the oven to 350ºF.

2. Put kale leaves into a large plastic bag and add oil. Shake and then spread on a large baking sheet.

3. Bake within 12 minutes. Serve with salt.

Nutrition: Calories: 163- Fat: 10g

Protein: 2g- Net carbs: 14g

CONCLUSION

The ketogenic diet is the ultimate tool you can use to plan your future. Can you picture being more involved, more productive and efficient, and more relaxed and energetic? That future is possible for you, and it does not have to be a complicated process to achieve that vision. You can choose right now to be healthier and slimmer and more fulfilled tomorrow. It is possible with the ketogenic diet.

When people get older, their bones weaken. At 50, your bones at likely not as strong as they used to be. However, you can keep them in really good conditions. Consuming milk to give calcium cannot do enough to strengthen your bones.

Whether you have met your weight loss goals, your life changes, or you simply want to eat whatever you want again. You cannot just suddenly start consuming carbs again, for it will shock your system. Have an idea of what you want to allow back into your consumption slowly. Be familiar with portion sizes and stick to that amount of carbs for the first few times you eat post-keto.

Dealing with weight issues can be disheartening, and you do not have to be extremely overweight or obese to feel the effects. These extra pounds can put a strain on your overall health and wellness. They can make you less efficient in your work life and everyday activities. They can take you away from the things you like to do and the places you love to visit. They can make you feel winded and out of breath at the simplest activities. They can take away your joy of living life to the fullest.

The things to watch out for when coming off keto are weight gain, bloating, more energy, and feeling hungry. The weight gain is nothing to freak out over; perhaps you might not even gain any. It all depends on your diet, how your body processes carbs, and of course, water weight. The length of your keto diet is a significant factor in how much weight you have lost caused by the reduction of carbs. The bloating will occur because of the reintroduction of fibrous foods and your body getting used to digesting them again. The bloating van lasts for a few days to a few weeks. You will feel like you have more energy because carbs break down into glucose, which is the body's primary source of fuel. You may also notice better brain function and the ability to work out more.

Start with non-processed carbs like whole grain, beans, and fruits. Start slow and see how your body responds before resolving to add carbs one meal at a time.

This is not a fancy diet that promises falsehoods of miracle weight loss. This diet is proven by years of science and research, which benefits not only your waistline, but your heart, skin, brain, and organs. It does not just improve your physical health, but your mental and emotional health as well. This diet improves your health holistically.